Discarded

A Look at
Renaissance Art

Written by
J. Jean Robertson

rourkeeducationalmedia.com

www.rourkeeducationalmedia.com

PHOTO CREDITS: Cover: © Lucian Milasan (bottom), © DHuss (statue); page 1: © snem; page 3: © Antonel; page 8: © sedmak; page 12: © marcoprati; page 13: © Alysta; page 18: © Imaengine; page 19: © peterspiro, © DHuss (statue)

Edited by Precious McKenzie

Cover and Interior design by Tara Raymo

Library of Congress PCN Data

A Look at Renaissance Art / J. Jean Robertson
 (Art and Music)
  ISBN 978-1-62169-874-6 (hard cover)
  ISBN 978-1-62169-769-5 (soft cover)
  ISBN 978-1-62169-974-3 (e-Book)
Library of Congress Control Number: 2013936783

Rourke Educational Media
Printed in the United States of America,
North Mankato, Minnesota

Also Available as:

Educational Media

rourkeeducationalmedia.com

customerservice@rourkeeducationalmedia.com • PO Box 643328 Vero Beach, Florida 32964

Table of Contents

What is the Renaissance?

What does renaissance mean? The word renaissance is a French word which means rebirth, or born again. **Renaissance** is a name given to a rapidly changing time in history.

What made the Renaissance happen? As people studied and experimented, a new way of thinking developed. It was called **Humanism**. People began to think more about making life better and more enjoyable for others.

The Magpie on the Gallows by Pieter Bruegel the Elder, 1568.

During this time, individuals became more important than churches, kings, and royalty.

The Marriage Feast at Cana by Hieronymus Bosch, after 1550.

The New Art

The city of Florence, Italy is considered the birthplace of Renaissance art.

Renaissance art eventually moved throughout Italy and into northern Europe.

Melancholy by Lucas Cranach the Elder, 1532.

St. Mark by Donatello, 1411–1413.

Renaissance artists used new techniques to make their **sculptures** and paintings more realistic.

Three dimensional paintings were prized as the only way to have realistic pictures of people because photography had not yet been invented.

Compare the two Madonna paintings. Which looks more life-like?

Madonna and Child Enthroned by Cimabue, 1280-1285.

Madonna in Maest by Giotto, 1310.

Painters began using **perspective** and shadows to give the feeling of three dimensions to a flat painting. This was called **realism**.

The Court Scene at the Camera degli Sposi commissioned by Ludovico III Gonzaga painted by Andrea Mantegna, between 1465 and 1474.

Since Humanism was a different way of thinking, it influenced changes in many areas. Changes happened in architecture, literature, music, and science.

People with wealth paid artists to compose and perform music, design buildings, and create sculptures and paintings.

*The Arnolfini Marriage
by Jan van Eyck, 1434.*

Renaissance art is often divided into two time periods:
Early Renaissance and High Renaissance. The architect
Filippo Brunelleschi led other artists by using the
classical principles of balance, simplicity, and restraint
in his creations.

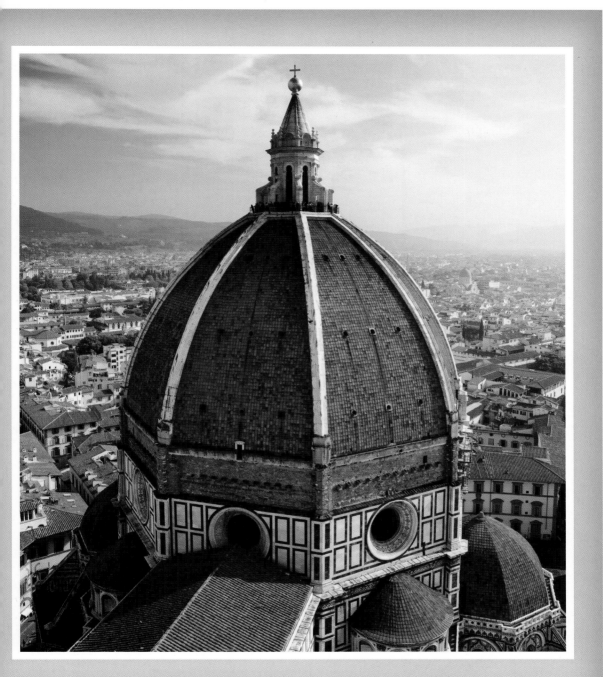

Brunelleschi designed the dome of the Florence Cathedral using the mathematical principles of proportion, symmetry, and simplicity. It is conical in shape, with eight sides, and is supported by eight ribs which can be seen both inside and outside. Between the inner and outer shells are sixteen, unseen, smaller ribs. A lantern tops the dome for beauty and support. Brunelleschi's masterpiece still stands in Florence, Italy.

The Annunciation by Sandro Botticelli, 1489-1490.

Most early art was religious art. Religious art continue
to be important during the Renaissance, but **secular**, no
religious, art began to be important.

Giotto di Bondone, usually called just Giotto, was one of the first Renaissance painters. Many other painters followed his example of painting things as they really looked.

Kiss of Judas by Giotto, 1304-1306.

The High Renaissance

Raphael 1483-152[

The School of Athens, 1509–1510.

The Early Renaissance techniques were followed and refined by artists in the High Renaissance period. Three names stand out among the many High Renaissance artists: Raphael, Michelangelo, and Leonardo.

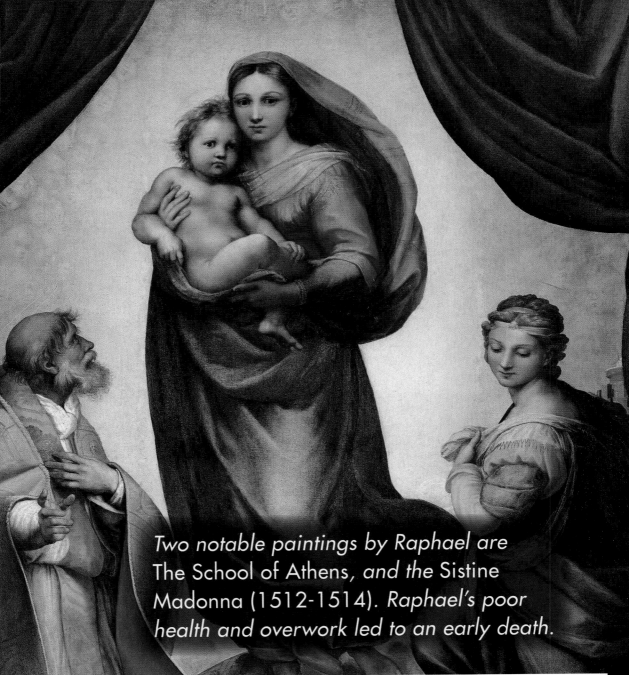

Two notable paintings by Raphael are The School of Athens, *and the* Sistine Madonna (1512-1514). *Raphael's poor health and overwork led to an early death.*

Raphael was very careful with his work, and faithful in doing what he promised to do. He created both small and large paintings. The people in his paintings looked almost alive.

Michelangelo is renowned for his painting of the ceiling of the Sistine Chapel. He painfully painted the entire huge ceiling lying on his back. It took four years.

Sistine Chapel, 1508–1512.

Michelangelo was a gifted architect, sculptor, and painter. He preferred sculpting to painting. He designed the Dome of St. Peter's Cathedral. His most famous sculpture is the eighteen foot (5.5 meter) tall statue of David carved from a single piece of marble.

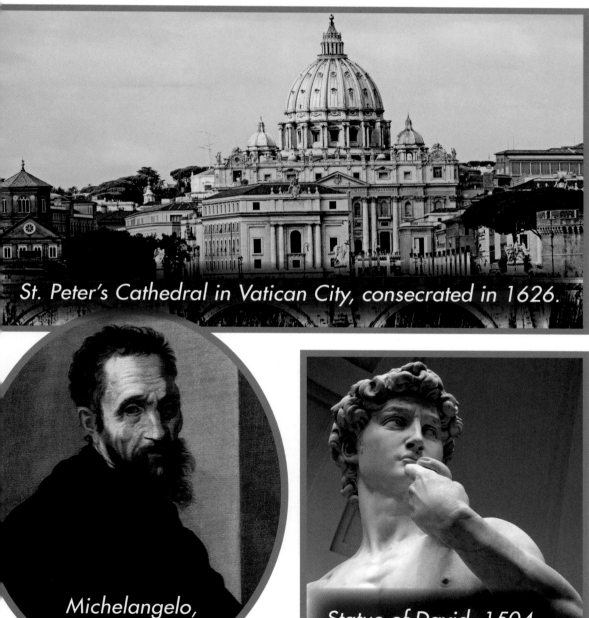

St. Peter's Cathedral in Vatican City, consecrated in 1626.

Michelangelo, 1475-1564.

Statue of David, 1504.

Leonardo da Vinci, 1452-1519.

Vitruvian Man, 1490.

The Last Supper, 1495–1498.

Leonardo da Vinci, often called just Leonardo, was "The Ultimate Renaissance Man" because he was good a everything. Leonardo was an artist, scientist, and invento

He had so many talents and interests that he had difficulty finishing all his projects. Many were never completed. Two of his most famous paintings are *The Las Supper* and the *Mona Lisa*.

Mona Lisa, 1503–1506.

St. Helena by Cima da Conegliano, 149[?]

You may wonder how Renaissance art and artists have benefited our world today. In addition to many beautiful works of art, they have shown us that we can find new ways of doing things. They have also shown us the value and beauty found in hard work.